THE POWER OF PERSONAL DEVELOPMENT

CULTIVATING HABITS AND MINDSETS FOR SUCCESS

PARTHASARATHY G

Made with ♥ on the Notion Press Platform
www.notionpress.com

Dedicated to friends and family...

Contents

Contents

Acknowledgements

Thank you, dear reader and friend, for choosing to read **"The Power of Personal Development: Cultivating habits and mindsets for success".**

I would like to express my gratitude to everyone who supported me in writing this book.

First and foremost, I would like to thank Rahul, my first reader, for his invaluable feedback.

I would also like to thank my friends and family who have made life worth living. A special shoutout to my extended family on Instagram, Twitter, and Facebook for their constant support.

Last but not least, I want to express my appreciation to the entire team at NotionPress Publications and Amazon kdp for their hard work in bringing this book to life.

Welcome to "The Power of Personal Development: Cultivating habits and mindsets for success". I hope you enjoy reading it as much as I enjoyed writing it.

Introduction

Personal development is the process of improving oneself through various means, such as education, self-help, and professional development. It involves the conscious effort to enhance one's knowledge, skills, and attitudes to become a better person and achieve one's goals.

In today's fast-paced world, personal development has become more important than ever. With the constant changes and challenges that we face in our personal and professional lives, it is essential to have the right mindset and skills to succeed.

Personal development is crucial for several reasons. Firstly, it helps us to develop a sense of purpose and direction in life. When we have a clear idea of what we want to achieve, we are more likely to take action towards our goals and make better decisions.

Secondly, personal development helps us to develop the necessary skills and knowledge to succeed in our personal and professional lives. By continuously learning and improving ourselves, we can become better communicators, problem-solvers, and leaders.

Thirdly, personal development helps us to cultivate a positive mindset and attitude towards life. When we have a positive outlook, we are more resilient, able to bounce back from setbacks, and enjoy a better quality of life.

In this book, we will explore why personal development matters and provide actionable advice and strategies to help you develop the habits and mindsets necessary for success. We will cover topics such as self-awareness, goal-setting, mindset, discipline, resilience, communication, leadership, and continuous learning.

In the following chapters, we will examine the key elements of personal development, exploring the habits and mindsets that successful people use to achieve their goals and reach their full potential. We will provide practical advice and tools that you can use to develop these habits and mindsets in your own life, helping you to create a roadmap for personal growth and development.

Throughout this book, we will emphasize the importance of self-awareness, which is the foundation of personal development. We will explore the different aspects of self-awareness, including emotional intelligence, self-reflection, and mindfulness, and provide strategies to help you develop these skills.

We will also look at the importance of discipline and habits in personal development. Habits are the building blocks of success, and developing positive habits is crucial to achieving our goals. We will provide advice and tools to help you develop positive habits and break negative ones.

Goal-setting is another critical aspect of personal development, and we will explore different methods for setting and achieving goals. We will examine the importance of having a clear purpose and direction in life and show you how to align your goals with your values.

Communication skills are also crucial for personal development, and we will explore different techniques for effective communication, including active listening, empathy, and assertiveness. We will examine the importance of building strong relationships and show you how to develop your communication skills to build better connections with others.

Resilience is another key aspect of personal development, and we will examine strategies for bouncing back from setbacks and challenges. We will explore the importance of positive thinking and gratitude in developing resilience, and provide advice on how to cultivate a positive mindset.

Finally, we will look at the importance of continuous learning and growth in personal development. Learning is a lifelong process, and developing a love of learning is essential to achieving success. We will explore different methods for continuous learning, including reading, listening to podcasts, and attending workshops and conferences.

In conclusion, personal development is essential for achieving success and leading a fulfilling life. By developing the habits and mindsets necessary for personal growth and development, we can achieve our goals, overcome obstacles, and lead a happier and more fulfilling life. In the following chapters, we will explore the key elements of personal development and provide practical advice and strategies to help you develop these habits and mindsets in your own life.

ONE

The Growth Mindset: How Your Beliefs Affect Your Success

Have you ever felt stuck in your personal or professional life, unable to make progress towards your goals? Do you struggle with self-doubt and fear of failure? If so, you are not alone. Many people experience these challenges at some point in their lives, and often the root cause is their mindset.

The concept of mindset has been around for centuries, but it was popularized by psychologist Carol Dweck in her book "Mindset: The New Psychology of Success." In her book, Dweck introduced the concept of fixed and growth mindsets, two different beliefs about intelligence and abilities that can have a profound impact on our success.

A fixed mindset is the belief that intelligence and abilities are fixed traits that cannot be changed. People with a fixed mindset often believe that their success or failure is determined by their innate abilities and talent, rather than their effort and hard work. They may avoid challenges and feel threatened by feedback or criticism, fearing that it will expose their limitations.

On the other hand, a growth mindset is the belief that intelligence and abilities can be developed through effort and practice. People with a growth mindset see challenges as opportunities for growth and learning, and they embrace feedback and criticism as a way to improve. They are more resilient and persistent in the face of setbacks, seeing them as temporary obstacles that can be overcome with effort and perseverance.

The good news is that mindset is not a fixed trait. It is a belief that can be changed and developed over time. By cultivating a growth mindset, you can transform your beliefs about yourself and your abilities, and unleash your full potential for success.

In this chapter, we will explore the concept of the growth mindset, and how it affects your success in life. We will examine the characteristics of a growth mindset, and provide practical strategies for developing this mindset in your own life.

The Characteristics of a Growth Mindset

People with a growth mindset possess several key characteristics that set them apart from those with a fixed mindset. These characteristics include:

A willingness to learn: People with a growth mindset are open to learning new things and developing new skills. They see every challenge as an opportunity to learn and grow.

A belief in the power of effort: People with a growth mindset believe that effort and hard work are the keys to success. They are willing to put in the time and effort required to achieve their goals.

A focus on progress: People with a growth mindset focus on progress, rather than perfection. They see setbacks and mistakes as opportunities to learn and improve.

A belief in their ability to change: People with a growth mindset believe that they can change and develop their abilities over time. They are not limited by their current abilities or circumstances.

A willingness to take risks: People with a growth mindset are willing to take risks and try new things, even if they might fail. They see failure as a natural part of the learning process, and are not afraid of making mistakes.

Developing a Growth Mindset

If you currently have a fixed mindset, don't worry. You can develop a growth mindset with practice and effort. Here are some strategies for cultivating a growth mindset:

Embrace challenges: Instead of avoiding challenges, embrace them as opportunities for growth and learning. Seek out challenges that will push you out of your comfort zone and help you develop new skills.

View setbacks as temporary: When you encounter setbacks or failures, don't give up. View them as temporary obstacles that can be overcome with effort and persistence.

Focus on the process: Instead of focusing on the end result, focus on the process of learning and improving. Celebrate small successes along the way, and don't get discouraged by setbacks.

TWO

Habits of Successful People: The Power of Daily Rituals

Have you ever wondered how successful people manage to achieve so much in their lives? What sets them apart from others? The answer lies in their habits and daily rituals.

Habits are the actions and behaviours that we repeat on a daily basis without even thinking about them. They are the foundation of our daily lives, and they have a powerful impact on our success and happiness. Successful people understand the importance of habits, and they intentionally cultivate daily rituals that support their goals and aspirations.

In this chapter, we will explore the habits and daily rituals of successful people, and how you can adopt these habits to achieve your own goals.

The Power of Daily Rituals

A daily ritual is a set of habits or actions that you perform at the same time each day. Daily rituals have several benefits, including:

Consistency: Daily rituals help you develop consistency and routine in your life, which can lead to increased productivity and success.

Focus: Daily rituals help you stay focused on your goals and priorities, and avoid distractions and procrastination.

Mindfulness: Daily rituals can be a form of mindfulness practice, helping you stay present in the moment and cultivate a sense of calm and peace.

Self-care: Daily rituals can be a form of self-care, helping you prioritize your physical and mental well-being.

Motivation: Daily rituals can help you stay motivated and committed to your goals, by creating a sense of momentum and progress.

Habits of Successful People

what are the habits and daily rituals of successful people? Here are some of the most common ones:

Wake up early: Many successful people wake up early to start their day with intention and focus. Waking up early allows them to have more time for self-care, exercise, and reflection before the demands of the day begin.

Exercise: Exercise is a common daily ritual among successful people, as it helps them maintain physical and mental health, and improve their focus and productivity.

Meditation or mindfulness practice: Many successful people practice meditation or mindfulness as a way to reduce stress and improve their mental clarity and focus.

Gratitude practice: Practicing gratitude is a powerful daily ritual that can help you cultivate a positive mindset and increase your overall well-being.

Planning and goal-setting: Successful people often take time each day to plan and set goals, to ensure that they are focused on their priorities and making progress towards their aspirations.

Reading or learning: Successful people prioritize learning and personal growth, often by reading or listening to books, podcasts, or other educational materials.

Reflection: Daily reflection is a common practice among successful people, as it helps them assess their progress, identify areas for improvement, and stay focused on their goals.

Adopting Daily Rituals

If you want to adopt daily rituals that support your goals and aspirations, here are some tips to get started:

Start small: Begin by adopting one or two daily rituals that are manageable and achievable, and build on them over time.

Be intentional: Choose rituals that align with your values and priorities, and that will help you achieve your goals.

Be consistent: Consistency is key when it comes to developing daily rituals. Try to perform your rituals at the same time each day, and stick to them even when it's difficult.

Be flexible: While consistency is important, it's also important to be flexible and adapt your rituals as needed. If something isn't working, don't be afraid to make changes.

Track your progress: Keep track of your daily rituals and the progress you're making towards your goals. This can help you stay motivated and committed to your habits.

In conclusion, habits and daily rituals play a crucial role in the success of individuals, both in personal and professional domains. The habits that we cultivate and the daily routines that we follow have a profound impact on our mindset, productivity, and overall well-being. By adopting the habits of successful people and incorporating them into our daily lives, we can achieve our goals and reach our full potential.

However, it's important to note that forming new habits and routines is not always easy, and it requires discipline, patience, and consistency. It's essential to start with small and achievable goals, and gradually build upon them over time. It's also crucial to understand that everyone's journey is different, and what works for one person may not work for another.

Ultimately, the power of daily rituals lies in their ability to transform our lives by changing our mindset, our actions, and our outcomes. By making conscious choices about our habits and daily routines, we can create a life that is fulfilling, productive, and successful.

THREE

Goal Setting: How to Define and Achieve Your Objectives

Goal setting is a crucial step in achieving success in any aspect of life. Whether it's personal or professional goals, having a clear understanding of what you want to achieve and how to achieve it is essential. In this chapter, we will explore the process of goal setting, including how to define your objectives, create an action plan, and track your progress towards success.

Defining Your Objectives:

The first step in goal setting is to define your objectives clearly. This includes identifying what you want to achieve, why you want to achieve it, and how you plan to achieve it. To do this effectively, it's important to follow the SMART framework, which stands for Specific, Measurable, Achievable, Relevant, and Time-bound.

Specific goals are those that are clear and well-defined. Measurable goals have a quantifiable outcome, which allows you to track your progress. Achievable goals are those that are realistic and within your reach. Relevant goals are aligned with your values, vision, and purpose. Time-bound goals have a deadline or target date for completion.

Creating an Action Plan:

Once you have defined your objectives, the next step is to create an action plan. This involves breaking down your goals into smaller, manageable tasks and outlining the steps required to achieve each task. It's essential to prioritize your tasks based on their importance and urgency, and to allocate sufficient time and resources to each task.

Tracking Your Progress:

Tracking your progress is crucial to ensure that you are on track to achieving your objectives. This involves regularly reviewing your action plan, measuring your progress towards each task, and making adjustments as necessary. It's essential to celebrate your successes along the way and to stay motivated and focused on your end goal.

Overcoming Challenges:

Goal setting is not always an easy process, and there are many challenges that can arise along the way. These challenges may include lack of motivation, self-doubt, distractions, and setbacks. It's important to have a plan in place to overcome these challenges, such as seeking support from friends or colleagues, setting reminders, or revisiting your action plan.

Goal setting is a critical step towards achieving success in any area of life. By following the SMART framework, creating an action plan, tracking your progress, and overcoming challenges, you can achieve your objectives and reach your full potential. It's essential to be flexible and adaptable in your approach and to celebrate your successes along the way. Remember, the journey towards success is just as important as the destination.

FOUR

Mindfulness and Self-Awareness: Cultivating Inner Peace and Resilience

Mindfulness and self-awareness are essential skills for cultivating inner peace and resilience. In today's fast-paced world, it's easy to get caught up in the chaos and distractions of everyday life, and to lose touch with our inner selves. In this chapter, we will explore the benefits of mindfulness and self-awareness, including how they can help us to manage stress, improve our relationships, and enhance our overall well-being.

The Power of Mindfulness:

Mindfulness is the practice of being present in the moment, without judgment or distraction. It involves paying attention to our thoughts, feelings, and sensations, and observing them without reacting to them. Mindfulness has been shown to have many benefits, including reducing stress and anxiety, improving mental clarity, and enhancing our overall sense of well-being.

The Importance of Self-Awareness:

Self-awareness is the ability to recognize and understand our own thoughts, emotions, and behaviours. It's a critical skill for personal growth and development, as it allows us to identify our strengths and weaknesses, and to make positive changes in our lives. Self-awareness also helps us to develop empathy and compassion for others, as we become more attuned to their feelings and perspectives.

Practicing Mindfulness and Self-Awareness:

There are many ways to practice mindfulness and self-awareness, including meditation, yoga, and journaling. These practices can help us to cultivate a deeper sense of inner peace and resilience, and to develop a greater sense of connection with ourselves and others. It's essential to find a practice that works for us, and to make it a regular part of our daily routine.

Benefits of Mindfulness and Self-Awareness:

The benefits of mindfulness and self-awareness are numerous, and they extend beyond our personal lives into our professional and social relationships. By developing these skills, we can become more effective communicators, better problem-solvers, and more empathetic and compassionate individuals. We can also become more resilient in the face of challenges and setbacks, and more capable of managing stress and anxiety.

In conclusion, cultivating mindfulness and self-awareness is a critical step towards achieving inner peace and resilience. By practicing these skills regularly, we can improve our overall well-being, enhance our personal and professional relationships, and develop a greater sense of empathy and compassion for others. It's essential to make these practices a regular part of our daily routine, and to stay committed to our personal growth and development.

FIVE

Overcoming Limiting Beliefs: How to Change Your Inner Dialogue

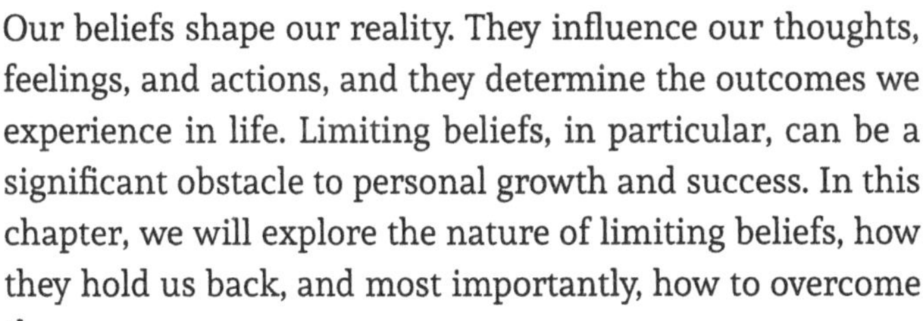

Our beliefs shape our reality. They influence our thoughts, feelings, and actions, and they determine the outcomes we experience in life. Limiting beliefs, in particular, can be a significant obstacle to personal growth and success. In this chapter, we will explore the nature of limiting beliefs, how they hold us back, and most importantly, how to overcome them.

What are Limiting Beliefs?

Limiting beliefs are negative thoughts or assumptions that we hold about ourselves, others, or the world around us. They are often based on past experiences or social conditioning and can be deeply ingrained in our subconscious minds. Common examples of limiting beliefs include "I'm not smart enough," "I don't deserve happiness," or "I'm too old to change."

How Limiting Beliefs Hold Us Back:

Limiting beliefs can prevent us from reaching our full potential by creating self-imposed limitations. They can lead to self-doubt, fear, and anxiety, which can paralyze us and prevent us from taking action towards our goals. Limiting beliefs can also cause us to seek out evidence that confirms our negative self-perceptions, while discounting or ignoring evidence to the contrary.

Overcoming Limiting Beliefs:

Overcoming limiting beliefs requires a conscious effort to change our inner dialogue. It involves challenging our negative thoughts and assumptions, and replacing them with more positive and empowering beliefs. This process requires self-awareness, self-compassion, and a willingness to step outside our comfort zone.

Strategies for Overcoming Limiting Beliefs:

There are several strategies that we can use to overcome limiting beliefs, including:

Self-reflection: By examining our thoughts and beliefs, we can identify any limiting beliefs that may be holding us back.

Challenging negative self-talk: We can challenge our negative self-talk by questioning its validity and replacing it with more positive self-talk.

Reframing: Reframing involves looking at a situation from a different perspective, which can help us to see things in a more positive light.

Visualization: Visualization involves imagining ourselves achieving our goals, which can help to build confidence and motivation.

Action: Taking action towards our goals, even in small steps, can help to build confidence and challenge our limiting beliefs.

Benefits of Overcoming Limiting Beliefs:

By overcoming limiting beliefs, we can unlock our full potential and achieve greater success and happiness in life. We can build confidence, resilience, and a more positive self-image. We can also experience greater freedom and fulfillment by letting go of our self-imposed limitations.

In conclusion, overcoming limiting beliefs is a critical step towards personal growth and success. By changing our inner dialogue and challenging our negative thoughts and assumptions, we can unlock our full potential and achieve our goals. It's essential to stay committed to this process and to seek out support and guidance when needed. With patience, self-compassion, and a willingness to take action, we can overcome our limiting beliefs and live a more fulfilling life.

SIX

Time Management: Strategies for Boosting Productivity and Efficiency

Time management is a crucial skill that can help individuals achieve success in both their personal and professional lives. Effective time management involves prioritizing tasks, minimizing distractions, and allocating time to the activities that matter most. In this chapter, we will explore strategies for boosting productivity and efficiency through effective time management.

The Importance of Time Management:

Time is a finite resource, and how we use it can significantly impact our success and well-being. Poor time management can lead to missed deadlines, increased stress, and reduced productivity. On the other hand, effective time management can improve our focus, reduce stress, and increase our productivity, allowing us to achieve our goals and maximize our potential.

Strategies for Effective Time Management:

Set Goals: Setting clear, specific goals is a critical first step in effective time management. Knowing what you want to achieve can help you prioritize your tasks and allocate your time more efficiently.

Prioritize Tasks: Prioritizing tasks involves identifying which activities are most important and which can wait. By focusing on the most critical tasks first, you can maximize your productivity and ensure that you achieve your most significant goals.

Create a Schedule: Creating a schedule can help you allocate your time effectively, ensuring that you have enough time to complete your tasks while still allowing time for self-care and other important activities.

Minimize Distractions: Distractions, such as social media, email, and phone calls, can significantly impact productivity. By minimizing these distractions, you can stay focused and productive throughout the day.

Take Breaks: Taking breaks is essential for maintaining productivity and avoiding burnout. Short breaks throughout the day can help you recharge and maintain your focus.

Delegate Tasks: Delegating tasks can free up time for more critical activities and ensure that tasks are completed efficiently and effectively.

Use Time Management Tools: Time management tools, such as calendars, to-do lists, and time-tracking software, can help you stay organized and on track throughout the day.

Benefits of Effective Time Management:

Effective time management can lead to several benefits, including:

Increased productivity: By focusing on the most critical tasks and minimizing distractions, you can increase your productivity and achieve your goals more efficiently.

Reduced stress: Effective time management can reduce stress by ensuring that you have enough time to complete your tasks and allowing time for self-care and other important activities.

Improved work-life balance: By allocating your time effectively, you can maintain a healthy work-life balance, ensuring that you have time for work, family, and other important activities.

Greater success: Effective time management can help you achieve your goals and maximize your potential, leading to greater success and fulfillment.

Effective time management is a critical skill that can help individuals achieve success in both their personal and professional lives. By setting clear goals, prioritizing tasks, minimizing distractions, and allocating time effectively, individuals can increase their productivity, reduce stress, and achieve their goals more efficiently. It's essential to stay committed to this process and to seek out support and guidance when needed. With patience, discipline, and a willingness to learn, individuals can master the art of time management and achieve their full potential.

SEVEN

Positive Thinking: The Power of Optimism and Gratitude

Positive thinking is a powerful tool that can help us overcome obstacles, manage stress, and achieve our goals. It is a mindset that is focused on looking for the good in every situation, and cultivating gratitude and optimism in our daily lives. In this chapter, we will explore the benefits of positive thinking and how you can incorporate this mindset into your life.

Benefits of Positive Thinking

Research has shown that positive thinking has numerous benefits for our mental and physical health. When we have a positive outlook on life, we are more likely to experience:

Reduced stress: Positive thinking can help us manage stress by shifting our focus from negative thoughts to more positive ones.

Improved relationships: People who have a positive mindset tend to have better relationships with others. This is because they are more likely to focus on the positive qualities of others, rather than their flaws.

Better mental health: Positive thinking has been linked to lower rates of depression and anxiety. This is because positive thinking can help us manage negative emotions and improve our overall mood.

Improved physical health: Positive thinking has been shown to have a positive effect on physical health. It can help reduce the risk of chronic diseases such as heart disease and diabetes, as well as improve our immune system.

Cultivating Positive Thinking

Cultivating a positive mindset takes practice and effort. Here are some strategies that you can use to cultivate positive thinking:

Gratitude: Focusing on the things that we are grateful for can help us maintain a positive mindset. You can start by writing down three things that you are grateful for every day.

Positive self-talk: The way we talk to ourselves can have a big impact on our mood and outlook on life. Replace negative self-talk with positive affirmations, such as "I am capable and strong."

Surround yourself with positivity: Spend time with people who have a positive mindset and avoid negative influences.

Visualize success: Visualizing success can help us stay motivated and focused on our goals. Take some time to visualize yourself achieving your goals and imagine how it will feel.

Incorporating positive thinking into your life can have a big impact on your overall well-being. By focusing on gratitude, positive self-talk, and visualizing success, you can cultivate a positive mindset and improve your mental and physical health. Remember that positive thinking takes practice and effort, but with time and dedication, you can develop a more positive outlook on life.

EIGHT

Building Strong Relationships: Communication and Empathy Skills

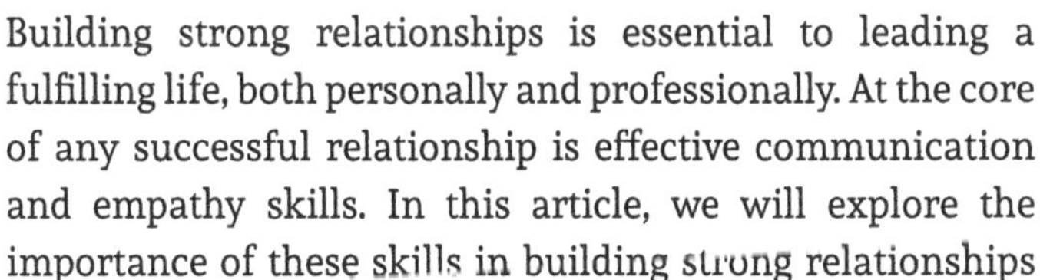

Building strong relationships is essential to leading a fulfilling life, both personally and professionally. At the core of any successful relationship is effective communication and empathy skills. In this article, we will explore the importance of these skills in building strong relationships and provide practical tips for improving them.

Communication Skills

Communication is the foundation of any relationship. It is the process by which we exchange information, ideas, and feelings with others. Good communication skills are essential in building strong relationships. Here are some tips for improving your communication skills:

Listen actively: Active listening means fully focusing on what the other person is saying without interrupting or judging them. It also involves giving feedback to show that you understand what they are saying.

Be clear and concise: Avoid using jargon or complicated words that the other person might not understand. Instead, use simple and clear language to convey your message effectively.

Use body language: Nonverbal communication is just as important as verbal communication. Use eye contact, facial expressions, and gestures to convey your message and show that you are engaged in the conversation.

Show empathy: Empathy is the ability to understand and share the feelings of others. When you show empathy, you are able to connect with others on a deeper level and build stronger relationships.

Use humour: Humour can help to diffuse tension and break the ice in difficult conversations. However, be careful not to use humour at the other person's expense, as this can damage the relationship.

Avoid blame and criticism: Blaming and criticizing others can be damaging to relationships. Instead, focus on finding solutions and working together to resolve any issues.

Ask questions: Asking questions shows that you are interested in the other person and want to understand their perspective. It can also help to clarify any misunderstandings and build stronger relationships.

Empathy Skills

Empathy is the ability to understand and share the feelings of others. It is a critical skill in building strong relationships, as it allows us to connect with others on a deeper level and understand their needs and concerns. Here are some tips for improving your empathy skills:

Practice active listening: Active listening involves fully focusing on what the other person is saying without interrupting or judging them. It also involves giving feedback to show that you understand what they are saying.

Put yourself in their shoes: Try to imagine how the other person is feeling and what their perspective might be. This can help you to understand their needs and concerns and build stronger relationships.

Validate their feelings: When someone shares their feelings with you, it is important to validate them. This means acknowledging their feelings and showing that you understand and care about them.

Show compassion: Compassion involves being kind, caring, and supportive towards others. When you show compassion, you are able to connect with others on a deeper level and build stronger relationships.

Be non-judgmental: Avoid judging others or making assumptions about their feelings or motivations. Instead, focus on understanding their perspective and building stronger relationships.

Use open-ended questions: Open-ended questions are questions that require more than a yes or no answer. They encourage the other person to share more about their thoughts and feelings and can help to build stronger relationships.

Practice self-reflection: Self-reflection involves examining your own thoughts and feelings and how they may impact your relationships with others. By practicing self-reflection, you can become more aware of your own biases and assumptions and build stronger relationships with others.

Building Strong Relationships

Building strong relationships requires a combination of effective communication and empathy skills. Here are some tips for building strong relationships:

Be present: When you are with someone, be fully present and engaged in the conversation. Avoid distractions like checking your phone or thinking about other things. This shows that you value the other person and their time.

Show appreciation: When someone does something kind or helpful for you, take the time to show your appreciation. This can be as simple as saying thank you or sending a heartfelt message.

Be authentic: Authenticity is key to building strong relationships. Be honest and genuine in your interactions with others, and don't be afraid to show your vulnerability.

Practice forgiveness: Everyone makes mistakes, and forgiveness is essential in building strong relationships. When someone apologizes for a mistake, accept their apology and move forward.

Communicate effectively: Effective communication is critical in building strong relationships. Use active listening, clear and concise language, and nonverbal communication to convey your message effectively.

Be open-minded: Be open to new ideas and perspectives, even if they differ from your own. This can help to build stronger relationships and lead to personal growth.

Prioritize your relationships: Building strong relationships takes time and effort. Prioritize your relationships by making time for the people who matter to you and showing them that they are important.

Effective communication and empathy skills are essential in building strong relationships. By practicing active listening, showing empathy, and prioritizing our relationships, we can connect with others on a deeper level and build stronger, more fulfilling relationships. Remember that building strong relationships takes time and effort, but the rewards are well worth it.

NINE

Leadership and Influence: How to Inspire and Motivate Others

Leadership and influence are two critical components of success in any organization. Effective leaders have the ability to inspire and motivate others to achieve their goals, while also driving the overall success of the organization. In this essay, we will explore the concept of leadership and influence, and discuss how to inspire and motivate others to achieve their full potential.

Understanding Leadership

Leadership is the ability to inspire and influence others to achieve a common goal. It involves setting a clear vision, providing direction, and creating a sense of purpose and motivation within the team. Here are some key characteristics of effective leaders:

Visionary: Effective leaders have a clear vision of where they want to take their team or organization. They are able to communicate this vision in a way that inspires and motivates others to work towards achieving it.

Communicative: Effective leaders are strong communicators. They are able to convey their message clearly and effectively to their team, and are also skilled at active listening.

Decisive: Leaders must make difficult decisions in a timely manner. Effective leaders are able to weigh the pros and cons of a situation and make a decision that is in the best interest of their team or organization.

Collaborative: Effective leaders are able to work collaboratively with their team to achieve their goals. They encourage teamwork and foster a sense of collaboration and cooperation.

Ethical: Effective leaders are committed to ethical behaviour and integrity. They set a positive example for their team and hold themselves to the highest ethical standards.

Empathetic: Effective leaders understand the needs and concerns of their team members. They are able to show empathy and understanding, and are supportive and encouraging.

Building Influence

Influence is the ability to affect the behaviour or opinions of others. Effective leaders must be able to build influence in order to motivate their team to achieve their goals. Here are some tips for building influence:

Lead by example: The best way to build influence is by leading by example. Be the change that you want to see in your team, and set a positive example for others to follow.

Communicate effectively: Effective communication is critical in building influence. Be clear and concise in your communication, and listen actively to others.

Build relationships: Building strong relationships with your team is essential in building influence. Take the time to get to know your team members and show that you care about them as individuals.

Be confident: Confidence is key to building influence. Be confident in your decisions and your ability to lead your team.

Show empathy: Empathy is important in building influence. Show that you understand and care about the needs and concerns of your team members.

Be consistent: Consistency is important in building influence. Be consistent in your behaviour and your decision-making, and be accountable for your actions.

Inspiring and Motivating Others

Inspiring and motivating others is essential in achieving success as a leader. Here are some tips for inspiring and motivating your team:

Set clear goals: Clear goals are essential in motivating your team. Set specific, measurable, achievable, relevant, and time-bound (SMART) goals that align with your team's overall vision.

Provide feedback: Feedback is essential in motivating your team. Provide regular feedback on performance, and recognize and celebrate successes.

Encourage growth and development: Encourage your team members to grow and develop their skills. Provide opportunities for training and development, and give your team members autonomy to take on new challenges.

Show appreciation: Show appreciation for your team members' hard work and dedication. Recognize their contributions and celebrate their successes.

Foster a positive culture: Foster a positive culture within your team. Encourage teamwork and collaboration.

TEN

Personal Growth and Continuous Learning: Embracing Change and Innovation

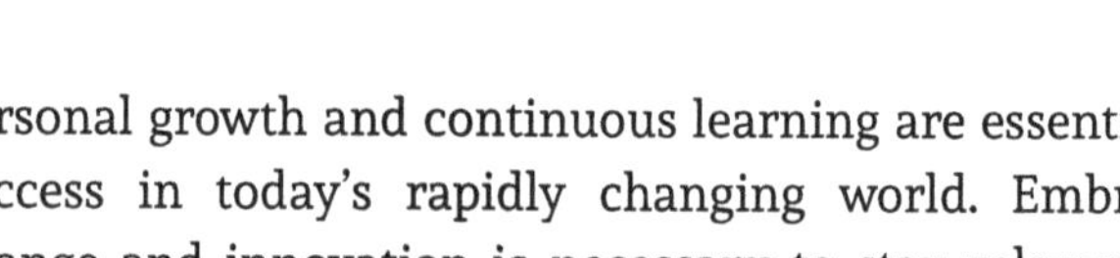

Personal growth and continuous learning are essential for success in today's rapidly changing world. Embracing change and innovation is necessary to stay relevant and competitive in any field. In this essay, we will explore the concept of personal growth and continuous learning, and discuss how to embrace change and innovation to achieve personal and professional success.

Understanding Personal Growth and Continuous Learning

Personal growth is the process of developing one's knowledge, skills, and abilities to reach their full potential. Continuous learning is the ongoing pursuit of knowledge and skill development throughout one's life. Here are some key characteristics of individuals who prioritize personal growth and continuous learning:

Curiosity: Individuals who prioritize personal growth and continuous learning are curious about the world around them. They seek out new knowledge and experiences to expand their understanding.

Open-mindedness: Personal growth and continuous learning require an open-minded approach. Individuals must be willing to consider new ideas and perspectives, and be open to change.

Self-awareness: Personal growth requires self-awareness. Individuals must be able to identify their strengths and weaknesses, and be willing to work on areas that need improvement.

Adaptability: Continuous learning requires adaptability. Individuals must be able to adapt to new technologies, processes, and methods in their field.

Resilience: Personal growth and continuous learning require resilience. Individuals must be able to bounce back from setbacks and challenges, and learn from their mistakes.

Embracing Change and Innovation

Embracing change and innovation is necessary for personal and professional growth. Here are some tips for embracing change and innovation:

Be proactive: Embrace change and innovation by taking a proactive approach. Seek out new technologies, processes, and methods in your field, and be willing to try new things.

Stay informed: Stay informed about changes and innovations in your field. Read industry publications, attend conferences and workshops, and network with others in your field.

Be adaptable: Embrace change and innovation by being adaptable. Be willing to adapt to new technologies, processes, and methods as they emerge.

Foster creativity: Foster creativity by seeking out new ideas and perspectives. Encourage brainstorming sessions and idea sharing with colleagues.

Embrace failure: Embrace failure as a learning opportunity. Understand that not every new idea or innovation will be successful, but that failure can provide valuable lessons for future growth and innovation.

Cultivating Personal Growth and Continuous Learning

Cultivating personal growth and continuous learning is essential for success in today's rapidly changing world. Here are some tips for cultivating personal growth and continuous learning:

Set goals: Set specific goals for personal growth and continuous learning. Identify areas where you want to improve your knowledge, skills, and abilities, and develop a plan to achieve those goals.

Prioritize learning: Prioritize learning by making it a regular part of your routine. Set aside time each day or week for reading, attending workshops, or pursuing other learning opportunities.

Seek feedback: Seek feedback from others to identify areas where you can improve. Be open to constructive criticism and use it to guide your personal growth and continuous learning.

Take risks: Take risks by pursuing new opportunities and trying new things. Step outside your comfort zone and embrace new challenges.

Practice reflection: Practice reflection by regularly reviewing your progress and evaluating your successes and failures. Use this reflection to guide your future learning and growth.

Personal growth and continuous learning are essential for success in today's rapidly changing world. By embracing change and innovation and cultivating personal growth and continuous learning, individuals can achieve their full potential and stay competitive in their field. Remember that personal growth and continuous learning require a proactive, open-minded approach, and a willingness to take risks and learn from failure. By adopting these approaches, individuals can develop the skills and knowledge they need to succeed in their personal and professional lives.

Personal growth and continuous learning are not a one-time event but rather an ongoing process. It requires individuals to embrace new experiences and ideas continuously, seek out opportunities for growth and development, and take risks to achieve their goals. By prioritizing personal growth and continuous learning, individuals can gain the knowledge, skills, and abilities needed to succeed in today's rapidly changing world.

In conclusion, personal growth and continuous learning are essential for individuals who want to succeed in their personal and professional lives. Embracing change and innovation, cultivating a proactive approach, and prioritizing learning are just a few ways to achieve personal growth and continuous learning. By taking these steps, individuals can develop the skills and knowledge needed to adapt to new challenges, stay relevant in their field, and achieve their full potential.

ELEVEN

THE JOURNEY OF PERSONAL DEVELOPMENT

Personal development is an ongoing journey that one must embark upon if they wish to improve their lives, achieve their goals, and become the best version of themselves. This journey is not a destination, but rather a process that requires a lifelong commitment to self-improvement and growth.

Throughout this journey, individuals will face challenges, obstacles, and setbacks, but it is these experiences that will help shape them into the person they are meant to be. In this conclusion, we will reflect on the journey of personal development and discuss some of the key takeaways and lessons learned.

One of the most important aspects of personal development is self-awareness. Self-awareness is the ability to recognize one's own thoughts, feelings, and behaviours, and how they impact the world around us. It is through self-awareness that individuals can identify their strengths and weaknesses, set realistic goals, and work towards improving themselves.

Another key aspect of personal development is goal setting. Setting goals helps individuals to stay focused and motivated on their journey towards self-improvement. Goals can be short-term or long-term, and can be related to any area of one's life, including career, health, relationships, and personal growth.

In addition to self-awareness and goal setting, personal development also involves developing positive habits and behaviours. Habits are the things we do on a daily basis, and they have a significant impact on our lives. By developing positive habits, such as exercising regularly, eating healthy, and practicing gratitude, individuals can improve their overall well-being and achieve their goals.

Another important aspect of personal development is self-care. Self-care refers to the practices and activities that individuals engage in to take care of their physical, emotional, and mental well-being. This includes things like getting enough sleep, eating healthy, practicing mindfulness, and taking time for oneself.

Throughout the journey of personal development, individuals will also face obstacles and setbacks. These challenges can be difficult to overcome, but they provide an opportunity for growth and learning. By facing challenges head-on and learning from them, individuals can become more resilient and better equipped to handle future obstacles.

Another important aspect of personal development is self-reflection. Self-reflection involves taking time to reflect on one's thoughts, feelings, and behaviours, and how they impact the world around us. It is through self-reflection that individuals can gain a deeper understanding of themselves and make positive changes in their lives.

Finally, personal development is a journey that never ends. It is a lifelong process of growth and self-improvement, and it requires a commitment to learning, self-reflection, and taking action. By embracing personal development as a journey rather than a destination, individuals can continue to learn and grow throughout their lives.

In conclusion, the journey of personal development is a lifelong process that requires a commitment to self-awareness, goal setting, positive habits and behaviours, self-care, resilience, self-reflection, and a willingness to learn and grow. It is through this journey that individuals can improve their lives, achieve their goals, and become the best version of themselves. So, let us all embrace personal development as a journey and commit to ongoing growth and self-improvement.

Conclusion: Embrace The Power Of Personal Development

In this book, we have explored the power of personal development and how cultivating habits and mindsets can lead to success in all areas of life. We have discussed the importance of setting goals, prioritizing self-care, and developing a growth mindset, among other key topics.

By embracing the power of personal development, individuals can gain the tools and knowledge needed to achieve their full potential. Whether it is pursuing a new career, improving relationships, or simply living a happier and more fulfilling life, personal development can help individuals overcome obstacles and achieve their goals.

However, personal development is not a one-time event but rather an ongoing process. It requires individuals to be committed to continuous learning, self-reflection, and taking action to achieve their goals. It may also require individuals to step outside their comfort zones and embrace new experiences and challenges.

In the end, the power of personal development lies in its ability to transform individuals and their lives. By cultivating habits and mindsets for success, individuals can become the best version of themselves and live a life filled with purpose, passion, and joy.

So, we encourage you to embrace the power of personal development and make it a lifelong pursuit. Set goals, prioritize self-care, develop a growth mindset, and take action to achieve your dreams. The journey of personal development is a rewarding one, and the possibilities for growth and success are endless.

References

Dweck, C. S. (2006). Mindset: The New Psychology of Success. New York: Ballantine Books.

Covey, S. R. (2004). The 7 Habits of Highly Effective People: Powerful Lessons in Personal Change. New York: Simon & Schuster.

Duckworth, A. L. (2016). Grit: The Power of Passion and Perseverance. New York: Scribner.

Goleman, D. (1998). Working with Emotional Intelligence. New York: Bantam Books.

Csikszentmihalyi, M. (1990). Flow: The Psychology of Optimal Experience. New York: Harper & Row.

Books By This Author

Habits Matter

Everyone living in the world has different habits and that is one of the important elements that make up their life. Repeating any action often is called habit.

Doing something over and over becomes easy and familiar. The more we repeat a habit, the easier and more permanent it becomes. This is the power of habit.

To live a happier, more fulfilling life, some changes in your regular habits are necessary. Habits can be good or bad. It is important to develop good habits and avoid bad ones. Good habits help you succeed in life.

In this book you will learn about some good and noble habits that will elevate you to greater place.

The Unlikely Lovebirds: The Unlikely Lovebirds

Rohit, a young man from India, moved to the United Kingdom to pursue a job. In a chance encounter at an art gallery, he met Sarah, an aspiring young woman from the UK. Despite their different backgrounds and language barriers, they formed a deep connection and fell in love.

As they navigated the challenges of a cross-cultural relationship, Rohit and Sarah's love grew stronger. They appreciated each other's differences and stood by each other, determined to make their love work despite their families' differing expectations and beliefs.

Their love story is one of two people from different worlds, who found each other in a foreign land and fell in love against all odds. It's a story of a love that transcended cultural differences and brought two families together, and one that will endure for a lifetime.

HOW TO IMPROVE KIDS' SELF MANAGEMENT SKILLS

To raise successful, happy, confident children, we need to teach them to do their job themselves. You cannot raise happy children by doing everything for children or by making their worlds easily and comfortably. You can raise happy children by encouraging them to pursue interests and goals.

For this self-Management skills are more important one. If they learn these skills before becoming teens, sure they going to win this world. In this book, explained detailly about importance of self -management skills and how we can improve kids' self-management skills. So, this will be a good parenting guide.

SOCIAL ISSUES IN INDIA AND TAMIL NADU

Social issues are considered important in competitive exams like UPSC and TNPSC because they help assess the candidate's understanding of the social and economic problems faced by the country and the various measures taken by the government to address these issues.

In these exams, questions on social issues can test a candidate's knowledge of various social welfare schemes, policies, and programs implemented by the government, and their impact on the target population. Understanding social issues is also important for candidates who are interested in public service and want to contribute to the development and progress of society.

Therefore, preparing for social issues is considered crucial for competitive exams like UPSC and TNPSC as it can help candidates score well in the general studies paper, demonstrate their understanding of the Indian society and polity, and improve their chances of getting selected for public service.

About The Author

Parthasarathy G is an Engineering Graduate from Tamilnadu, India with more than a decade of exposure to the IT industry. In addition to his profession, he is passionate about studying everything about humanities, life, and social science subjects. His books always talk about human life, good society, philosophy, and motivational things.

The author is currently living in Chennai, the capital city of Tamilnadu State and the gateway of the culture of South India.

❦❦❦

If you're not already following me on social media, you can check out my accounts at below where I post about my books...

Instagram: @sarathycreations

Twitter: @sarathy1210

❦❦❦

Printed by Libri Plureos GmbH in Hamburg, Germany